# Stealing HOME

## JACKIE ROBINSON: AGAINST THE ODDS

written by Robert Burleigh

illustrated by Mike Wimmer

A Paula Wiseman Book
Simon & Schuster Books for Young Readers
New York    London    Toronto    Sydney

Arms outstretched to keep
his delicate balance,

### THEN AND NOW

Glance at any major-league baseball game today. African-American (as well as Latino and Asian) players dot the field wherever you look. They are among the leading batters, the best pitchers, the most breathtaking base runners. It is impossible to imagine contemporary baseball without them.

Now turn back the clock to 1946—and look again. From Boston and New York to Chicago and St. Louis, major-league baseball was strictly a white player's game. True, the so-called Negro leagues fielded great teams, with some players later to be named Hall of Famers, but none of these all-stars received as much as a phone call from any major-league club.

Baseball, of course, was only a bite-size picture of mid-twentieth-century American life. By law and by custom, in the South and in the North, a great wall separated black people and white. Could this begin to change?

Enter Jackie Robinson.

number 42 dances his odd,
pigeon-toed dance off third base

### JACK OF ALL SPORTS

Jackie Robinson became a Hall of Fame *baseball* player. But that, as they say, is only the tip of the iceberg. People who saw him play say baseball wasn't even his strongest game! If he had been white, there is no doubt Robinson would have been signed by one of the National Football League teams in the 1940s. After a stellar career at Pasadena Junior College (1937–39), Jackie went on to UCLA and starred in football, basketball, baseball, and track. In fact, he was the first UCLA athlete to get a letter in four sports.

Robinson helped make UCLA a football powerhouse (1940–41). In the 1940 season the "Midnight Express" averaged more than ten yards a carry. Basketball? Well, he was the top scorer on the UCLA team during his two years there. As for track, he broke his brother Mack's broad-jump record by leaping more than twenty-five feet. Want more? Jackie—no doubt in his spare time—even won several local tennis and ping-pong tournaments. What's left to say?

and down the dirt-scumbled and chalk-lined path leading to home plate ninety feet away,

### "DEM BUMS" AIN'T BUMS NO MORE

An old nickname for the Brooklyn Dodgers was "The Bums." That's because in the early years the team lost a lot—and often looked comically bad in losing!

This changed with the arrival of Jackie Robinson. During Jackie's ten-year major-league career (1947–56), Brooklyn won six National League pennants and one World Series. And when they didn't win the pennant, the Dodgers were always close behind.

Jackie, of course, didn't do it alone. His Brooklyn teammates at different times included such baseball greats as Pee Wee Reese, Duke Snider, Gil Hodges, and Dixie Walker, along with fellow African Americans Don Newcombe and Roy Campanella.

as the packed, white-shirted crowd
wakes to a visible electricity,

### DODGERS VERSUS YANKEES: CLASSIC BATTLES!

Unfortunately for Brooklyn fans, the powerful Dodger teams of the late 1940s and early 1950s arose at the same time as a number of awesome New York Yankee teams. The Yankees were led first by the great Joe DiMaggio and later by the immortal Mickey Mantle.

Brooklyn met the Bronx Bombers in what were called Crosstown Classics in all six of Jackie Robinson's pennant-winning years. But only once, in 1955, did the Dodgers come home world champs, winning the series in seven games.

It was, in fact, in that very World Series that Jackie spectacularly stole home. It happened during game one. The Dodgers ended up losing the game, but many observers credit Jackie's base-running daring with inspiring his team to go on to ultimate victory.

and voices
call out call out call out
(*"Jackie! Jackie! Jackie!"*),

## "I'M LOOKING FOR A BALLPLAYER WITH GUTS ENOUGH *NOT* TO FIGHT BACK!"

It was August 28, 1945. Jackie Robinson sat across from Brooklyn Dodger general manager Branch Rickey.

During an intense two-hour meeting, Rickey had questioned Robinson on everything from his personal life to his belief in himself. He reminded Jackie that he would face many trials—indifference, hate, even physical abuse—during his first year in the major leagues. Rickey especially wanted one thing. He wanted Jackie to remain cool and calm at all times. Speaking forcefully, the older man uttered a strange, blunt statement: "I'm looking for a ballplayer with guts enough *not* to fight back!"

Was Jackie ready for this? For a moment, he was surprised. In the end, however, he agreed to be exactly the ballplayer Rickey was looking for.

Against all odds, a new baseball world was about to be born.

and the pitcher rocks
and bends and goes
into his slow, careful
windup,

### JACKIE IN CANADA

April 18, 1946. When the Montreal Royals opened their
season in New Jersey, more fans had bought tickets than
there were seats in the stadium! Jackie didn't disappoint.
He whacked out four hits (one a home run) and scored
four times in the Royals' first-game romp.

Robinson led his team to the International League
pennant and to victory in the Junior World Series.

Montreal fans loved him for his courage, his inven-
tive base running, and his will to win. They hailed him
after the final game and even followed him down the
street, still cheering. Sportswriter Sam Maltin wrote (in
a combination of wit and bitterness): "It was probably
the only day in history that a black man ran from a
white mob with love instead of lynching on its mind."

OLD JE          LE GUM

darting a quick glance
sideways,

### THE LONELY, TRIUMPHANT YEAR

1947. The season that was. There were catcalls, jeers, death
threats, vicious slurs from opposing dugouts, beanballs,
spikes aimed at his legs–but Jackie Robinson kept his
promise to Branch Rickey and endured it all.

And concentrate he did. Playing first base, Robinson batted .297 and was a key reason Brooklyn won the
National League pennant. Fans soon realized that Jackie
Robinson was a special talent destined to change baseball forever–even before he was named 1947 Rookie of
the Year.

Still, Jackie's Dodger teammates ranged from being
occasionally hostile to being mostly distant. On road trips,
and before and after games, Robinson kept mainly to
himself. Sportswriter Jimmy Canon, reviewing Jackie's
first months in the big leagues, called him "the loneliest
man I have ever seen in sports."

OLD JI    LE GUM

where the base runner on third starts and stops cold and starts again, bursting suddenly in two strides from absolute stillness to full speed,

### JACKIE'S GREATEST SEASON

Jackie's most difficult year was no doubt 1947—his rookie season. But if statistics tell the tale, his "career year" was 1949. Experience, self-confidence, and natural ability combined to help him put it all together.

The results? A batting average of .342, 124 runs batted in, 203 hits, and a league-leading 37 stolen bases—all adding up to Robinson's being named the National League's most valuable player. In addition, he was picked as the second baseman on the major-league all-star team. The only downside to Jackie's awesome season was the World Series, where the crosstown New York Yankees defeated his Brooklyn Dodgers, 4 games to 1.

OLD JU                    LE GUM

until there is nothing now
but the tiny ball

## HE "NEVER HAD IT MADE"

Robinson's autobiography is titled *I Never Had It Made*.
Truer words, one might say, were never spoken. Con-
sider Jackie's childhood. Born in 1919 in Georgia, Jack
Roosevelt Robinson was the youngest of five children
born to Mallie and Jerry Robinson. When Jackie was
just six months old, his father, a poor sharecropper, left
the family and never returned.

Jackie's mother decided to take her family from rural
Georgia to Pasadena, California. All aboard! Things were
better for black people in California than in the South. But
not by that much. The family found it difficult to rent a
house. Food was often scarce. The children were called insulting names. Blacks were kept out of swimming pools, movie
theaters, and most restaurants. The miracle isn't that Jackie
Robinson became a baseball star. The miracle is that he kept
going.

OLD J    LE GUM

and the all-out sprinting man blurring toward the crouched catcher

## DAREDEVIL JACK

Jackie Robinson was an all-around baseball star. But it was on the base paths that he especially distinguished himself.

Keep in mind that from the 1920s on—mostly due to the influence of Babe Ruth—baseball had become more and more a power hitter's game. Base running had, to some extent, become a lost art.

Robinson helped change that. His ability to reach full speed in just a few strides, his instinct for taking an extra base, and his sheer speed made him a constant threat. He loved upsetting opposing pitchers into walking a batter or committing a balk. It was Jackie who, in the modern era, reopened the door to one of baseball's most exciting moments—bold base running. "Daring," he once declared; "that's half my game."

(the batter leaps backward
and away)

### MAN VERSUS BALL—MAN WINS!

Stealing home. On paper it looks like a hopeless proposition.
A major-league pitcher's fastball (coming roughly 60 feet from
the mound to home plate) arrives in less than one second.
The distance from third base to home plate is 90 feet, or 30
yards—a distance the world's fastest sprinters can't cover in
less than, say, three seconds. Add it up: No base runner from
third can ever beat the pitched ball to the plate.

But hold on. There is more. If the base runner is
alert, he can study the pitcher to detect that slight but all-
important pause between the windup and the release of
the ball; and if he is Jackie Robinson, he possesses the
quick start and gutsy attitude that make for a baseball
legend. Jackie stole home nineteen times in his career, most
notably during game one of the 1955 World Series.

OLD JI                    LE GUM

and then the wild,
dust-cloud–heaving
slide and quick foot
under the too-late tag

### WAKE UP, AMERICA:
### JACKIE CALLING

Jackie Robinson never willingly accepted being a second-class citizen.

Even as a youngster in Pasadena, he answered back to neighborhood children who taunted him with insulting names. One time he sat with friends at a local "whites only" lunch counter until they were finally served. As a college football player, he refused to stay in a different hotel from his white teammates. As a U.S. Army officer, he protested against the unfair treatment of black soldiers. For Jackie Robinson, the struggle never stopped.

Indeed, in his very last public interview (1972), sick and weak and dying, he called once again on organized baseball to admit African Americans to managerial and executive posts.

and the flat hands of the
umpire signaling *Safe*

### JACKIE THE MAGNET

Robinson endured insults from many opposing teams.
But he was also one of the most watched and most popular players of his time. During Jackie's first year in the
majors, Brooklyn Dodger attendance soared. Even when
the Dodgers played exhibition games in the South, thousands of black fans came early just to see infield practice!
In the late 1940s a movie was made of Jackie's life. (He
played himself.) One poll at the time named him America's
second most popular celebrity—after Bing Crosby.

Hank Aaron, Mister Home Run himself, recalls hear-
ing Jackie when he, Aaron, was a young man: "I think
he talked about segregation; but I didn't hear a word.
Jackie was such a hero to me—I couldn't do anything but
gawk."

One tribute—multiplied by thousands.

OLD JI                    BLE GUM

and the thunder of
screaming mouths,

### NOT BY MYSELF ALONE

When Jackie Robinson was inducted into baseball's Hall of Fame in 1962, three people shared the podium with him: Branch Rickey; Jackie's mother, Mallie; and his wife, Rachel.

To baseball watchers, Rickey was the best known of the three. But in many ways the two women were more important in Robinson's life.

His mother had more or less single-handedly raised five children. Her strong will and self-respect were part of Robinson's character all his life. His wife, Rachel (Jackie called her Rae), stood beside him from the time of their marriage in 1946 until his death in 1972. Her steady and quiet support helped Jackie endure the difficulties of his early baseball years. Rachel Robinson also had a significant career of her own, later teaching at the Yale University School of Nursing.

because this is Jackie Robinson, and baseball (and America, too) will never again be quite the same.

## JACKIE PLAYS ON

Jackie's late arrival on the big-league scene–he was twenty-eight as a rookie–cut his career short. He retired from baseball after playing for just ten years.

Jackie Robinson, however, never stopped moving ahead. For several years he worked as a business executive. At the same time he continued to fight against racism in his country. He befriended many activists, including Dr. Martin Luther King Jr.

Only poor health slowed Jackie down. Shortly before he died, the Dodgers–now the *Los Angeles* Dodgers–retired his old number, 42. (Later major-league baseball retired the number forever!) At the funeral the young reverend Jesse Jackson summed up the serious meaning of his life: "Jackie danced on the base paths," Jackson told the hushed crowd. "But it was more than a game."

For Barbara Kouts, with many thanks —R. B.

To all those who, like Jackie Robinson, realize that taking
what already belongs to you is not stealing. —M. W.

## Notes

p. 11, "I'm Looking for a Ballplayer With Guts Enough *Not* to Fight Back." Rickey quote from Rampersad, p. 126.

p. 13, "Jackie in Canada." Maltin quote from Rampersad, p. 157.

p. 15, "The Lonely, Triumphant Year." Canon quote from Rampersad, p. 172.

p. 21, "Daredevil Jack." Robinson quote from "Rookie of the Year."

For further information there are many interesting and informative
websites available, including the National Baseball Hall of Fame,
www.baseballhalloffame.org; www.JackieRobinson.com; and
www.baseballlibrary.com.

## Bibliography

Rampersad, Arnold. *Jackie Robinson*. New York: Knopf, 1997.

Robinson, Jackie. *I Never Had It Made*. As told to Alfred Duckett. New York: Putnam, 1972.

———. *Jackie Robinson's Little League Baseball Book*. Englewood Cliffs, NJ: Prentice Hall, 1972.

Robinson, Sharon. *Promises to Keep: How Jackie Robinson Changed America*. New York: Scholastic Press, 2004.

"Rookie of the Year." *Time*, September 27, 1947, http://www.time.com/time/magazine/article/0,9171,798173-1,00.html.

Simon, Scott. *Jackie Robinson and the Integration of Baseball*. Hoboken, NJ: John Wiley, 2002.

Tygiel, Jules, ed. *The Jackie Robinson Reader: Perspectives on an American Hero*. New York: Dutton, 1997.

 SIMON & SCHUSTER BOOKS FOR YOUNG READERS • An imprint of Simon & Schuster Children's Publishing Division
1230 Avenue of the Americas, New York, New York 10020 • Text copyright © 2007 by Robert Burleigh • Illustrations copyright © 2007 by Mike Wimmer
All rights reserved, including the right of reproduction in whole or in part in any form.
SIMON & SCHUSTER BOOKS FOR YOUNG READERS is a trademark of Simon & Schuster, Inc. • The text for this book is set in Berthold Baskerville.
The illustrations for this book are rendered in oil on canvas.
Manufactured in the United States of America • 10 9 8 7 6 5 4 3 2 1 • Library of Congress Cataloging-in-Publication Data • Burleigh, Robert.
Stealing home / Robert Burleigh ; Illustrated by Mike Wimmer.— 1st ed. • p. cm. • "A Paula Wiseman book." • ISBN-13: 978-0-689-86276-2
ISBN-10: 0-689-86276-8 • 1. Robinson, Jackie, 1919–1972–Juvenile literature.
2. Baseball players–United States–Biography–Juvenile literature. 3. African American baseball players–Biography–Juvenile literature. I. Wimmer, Mike. II. Title.
GV865.R6B87 2007
796.357092–dc22
2006001048

first
edition

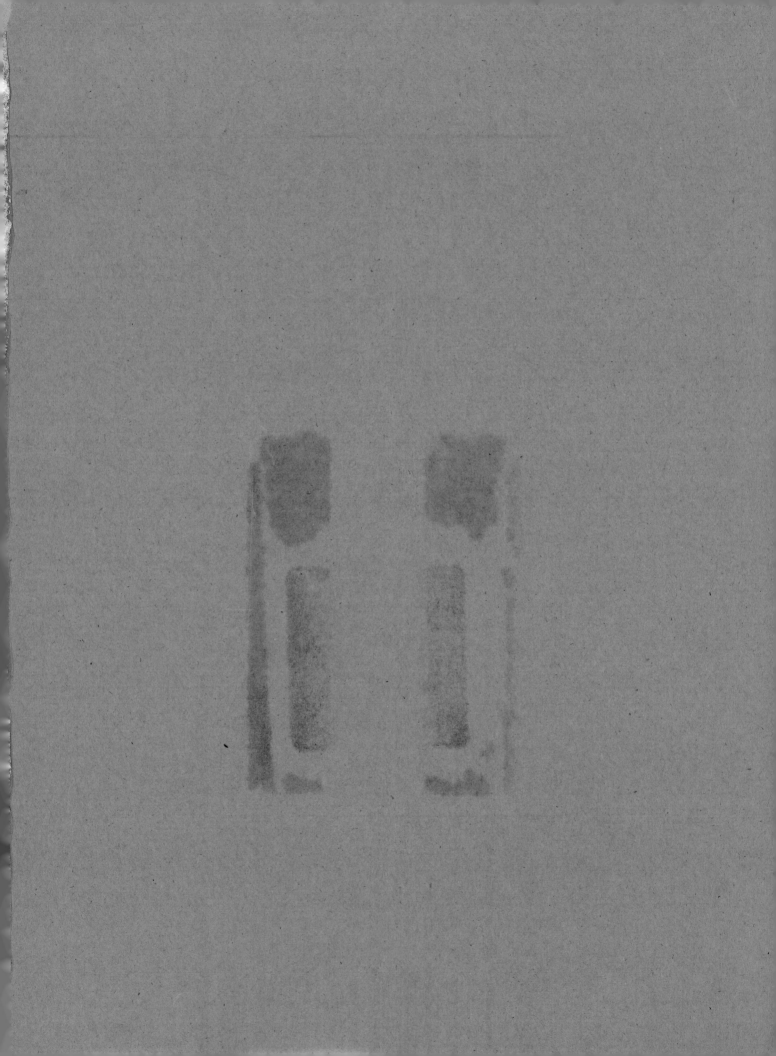

So they all sat under a tree and told Mr. Craven the story of the secret garden. And when they had told him everything, they all went back to the house together. Mary and Dickon ran ahead, while Colin and his father walked side by side, their heads in the air and their eyes full of laughter.

"Mary brought it to life," Dickon said.

"And Dickon and Colin, too," said Mary.

"And magic," said Colin.

"Tell me," said Mr. Craven.

The place was a wilderness of autumn gold and purple and violet blue
and flaming scarlet.

"I thought it would be dead," Mr. Craven said in wonder.

"I thought so too, at first," said Mary.

As he stood in front of the door, he thought he heard the sound of running feet and the laughter of children. Suddenly, a boy flung open the door and, without seeing Mr. Craven, dashed into his arms.

"Father!" the boy said, startled. "I am Colin."

"Take me into the garden, my boy," said his father, trembling with joy.

On the journey back he thought about his son. He had not meant to be a bad father, but he had missed his wife so much that he had not felt like a father at all. "I have been wrong in trying to forget about Colin," he thought. "Perhaps I can do him some good now."

As soon as he arrived at Misselthwaite, he made his way to the garden.

lake. He had a dream that his dear wife was calling to him, saying, "In the garden. In the garden!" When he woke, he felt happier than he had for years. "I must go back to Misselthwaite," he said.

While the secret garden was coming alive, Colin's father was wandering about the world. He visited beautiful places, but he was so sad that he never saw the beauty around him. Then one day he fell asleep beside a crystal blue

There was magic at work in the secret garden in the months that followed. The flowers grew as if fairies had planted them. And the roses! They came alive day by day, and Colin and Mary along with them. Colin decided that no one was to know he was getting stronger and stronger until he could walk and run like any other boy. This was to be the biggest secret of all, for Colin wanted to surprise his father.

Mary opened the door, and with one strong, splendid push from Dickon, Colin was in the secret garden. It was full of wonders that morning, and everywhere there were splashes of color and hummings and buzzings and scents.

"I shall get well!" Colin cried. He threw off the blanket covering his legs and gripped the arms of his chair.

"You can do it!" said Mary over and over again.

Dickon held Colin's arm; then Colin stretched out his thin legs and put his thin feet on the grass. He was standing! After a moment he took a few steps to a nearby tree, and though Dickon had to hold his arm, he was wonderfully steady.

So when the weather was warm enough, a footman carried Colin downstairs and outside and put him in his wheelchair. Dickon pushed the chair along while Mary walked beside it, and Colin lifted his face to the blue sky and breathed in the clear, sweet air. They wound in and out among the paths until at last they came to the garden door.

Colin was just like Mary, without friends to talk to or things to think about. He was always reading and looking at pictures in splendid books, and he had all sorts of wonderful puzzles to amuse himself with. But he was lonely and unhappy, and he liked the idea of a hidden garden as much as Mary. So he asked question after question about the garden until Mary finally said, "Perhaps, if you won't tell anyone, we can find out how to get into the garden by ourselves. And then, if we could find some strong boy to push you along in a wheelchair, we could go alone, just the three of us, and it would always be a secret garden."

"I never wanted to see anything before," said Colin, "but I want to see the secret garden."

Late that night Mary heard someone crying. She followed the sound down one corridor and another, until she came to a door that had a glimmer of light beneath it. She pushed it open. On the bed was a boy crying fretfully. When he saw Mary, he stopped crying and stared at her, his gray eyes wide with surprise.

"I am Colin Craven," he whispered at last. "Are you a ghost?"

"I am Mary Lennox. Mr. Craven is my uncle," Mary whispered back.

"He is my father," said the boy.

"No one ever told me he had a boy," gasped Mary.

"I am always ill and in bed, and I don't like people knowing about me and thinking I'm going to die," replied Colin.

"Does your father come and see you?" asked Mary curiously.

"Sometimes. My mother died soon after I was born, and it makes him sad to look at me." Colin looked angry for a moment.

"He shut up the garden because she died," said Mary, half to herself.

"What garden?" the boy asked.

"Oh, just a garden she liked," said Mary quickly.

"Tell me about the garden," said Colin.

"Will you come again and help me?" asked Mary when it was time for her to leave.

"I'll come every day," Dickon replied. "It's the best fun I've ever had—waking up a garden."

Mary and Dickon spent the afternoon going from bush to bush and from tree to tree, cutting away the dead rose branches to make room for the living ones. Then they planted the flower seeds Dickon had brought.

One morning on her way to the secret garden, Mary saw a boy sitting under a tree playing a wooden pipe. On the trunk of the tree he leaned against, a squirrel was watching him, and quite near him were two rabbits sitting up.

"I'm Dickon," the boy said when Mary came closer. "I've brought you some garden tools and seeds. Martha thought you might like them."

Mary decided that if the wild animals trusted Dickon, so could she.

"Come with me and I'll show you the secret garden," she said to Dickon, leading the way. "I'm the only one in the world who wants it alive."

She saw some pale green shoots sticking out of the earth. They seemed as if they were being choked by the grass, so she dug all around them. Every day after that Mary worked in the garden, feeling as happy and alive as the pale green shoots, which bloomed into crocuses and daffodils.

It was the sweetest, most mysterious-looking place anyone could imagine. Everywhere were bare branches of climbing roses, and the ground was covered with grass. It was different from any other place Mary had ever seen.

"Is it all quite dead?" she said softly, looking around and around.

One day Mary saw a robin hopping on the ground, looking for a worm. Mary looked down too, and noticed something almost buried in the soil. It was an old, rusty key.

"Perhaps it is the key to the garden," Mary said to herself.

A sudden gust of wind swung aside some ivy and uncovered a door hidden in a wall. Mary unlocked the door with her key and slowly pushed it open. She slipped through the door and shut it behind her. She was standing *inside* the secret garden.

Martha pointed the way to the gardens. "But there's one garden that
Mr. Craven locked up," she said. "It was his wife's garden and she loved it,
and when she died, he locked the door and buried the key. And no one's
gone in for years."

After that Mary could not stop thinking about the secret garden.

As soon as Mary arrived at Misselthwaite Manor, her uncle went away on business. There was nothing to do and no one to play with in the big, empty house. "Go outside," suggested Martha, the housemaid. "My brother Dickon spends hours by himself outside. That's how he made friends with the fox cub and the squirrels and the birds."

parents, for she had hardly known them. They had both been too busy to take care of her, so they had left her with servants who had given her everything she wanted. But she was very lonely.

THERE WAS ONCE A VERY SAD LITTLE GIRL NAMED MARY LENNOX. Mary's parents had died suddenly, and she was sent to Misselthwaite Manor to live with her uncle, Mr. Archibald Craven. Mary did not miss her

For Captain and Mrs. Moore
—M.C.

# The
# SECRET
# GARDEN

*Adapted from the original novel by*

FRANCES HODGSON BURNETT

*Illustrations by*

MARY COLLIER

■ HARPERCOLLINS*PUBLISHERS*

Text copyright © 1998 by HarperCollins Publishers • Text adapted by Alix Reid from *The Secret Garden* by Frances Hodgson Burnett • Illustrations copyright © 1998 by Mary Collier • All rights reserved. Printed in the U.S.A. • Library of Congress Cataloging-in-Publication Data • The secret garden / adapted from the original novel by Frances Hodgson Burnett ; illustrations by Mary Collier.    • p.    cm. • Summary:  In this abridged adaptation of the classic novel, a lonely orphan discovers the wonders of a mysterious garden and befriends her invalid cousin. • ISBN 0-06-027853-6 • [1. Orphans—Fiction. 2. Gardens—Fiction. 3. Physically handicapped—Fiction.] I. Collier, Mary, date, ill.   II. Burnett, Frances Hodgson, 1849–1924. Secret garden. • PZ7.S4475  1998 • 97-20757 • [E]—dc21 • CIP • AC • Typography by Alicia Mikles

And then everything happened at once.
A crowd of young girls, laughing and chattering,
came out of the palace and began running gaily
through the garden and down the steps.

"What did I tell you!" whispered Miriam.
"Here comes the princess! She's the tallest one!"
"She's seen the basket," said her mother softly.
"Look! She's sending a servant to fetch it!"

They hardly dared to look as the baby was laid in the princess's arms. He was crying.

"Isn't he beautiful?" the princess said. "He must be one of the Hebrew babies. Oh, poor little thing! He's hungry! He still needs his mother's milk."

Then Miriam stepped bravely out of the reeds and went straight up to the princess. She fell to her knees and said, "Your Highness, shall I call one of the slave women to come and nurse the baby for you?"

The princess smiled at Miriam. She seemed to understand.

"Yes, child, go," she said.

Miriam ran back and fetched her mother, who came and knelt before the princess.

"I will pay you to feed the child until he is old enough to come back to me," said the princess, placing the baby in his mother's arms. "Then I shall raise him as my own son. He will be a prince, and I shall call him Moses, because it means *Drawn from the water*."

When they were safely home again, Miriam's mother stared at her with tears of joy in her eyes.

"It all happened as you said it would!" she said.

"Yes," said Miriam.

And she picked up her drum and began to sing and dance,
just as she would do many years later, when Moses led the Hebrew
slaves out of Egypt into freedom in a land of milk and honey.